791.43   Funny!
FUN

$29.95

DATE			

12/15

Funny!

FUNNY!

Twenty-Five Years of Laughter from the Pixar Story Room

Foreword by **JOHN LASSETER**

Introduction by **JASON KATZ**

CHRONICLE BOOKS

SAN FRANCISCO

Library of Congress Cataloging-in-Publication Data is available.

ISBN: 978-1-4521-2228-1

Artists included in cover image collage: Erik Benson, Max Brace,
Jason Deamer, Harley Jessup, Jason Katz, Robert Lence, Matthew
Luhn, Patrick McDonnell, Teddy Newton, Bob Pauley, Jeff Pidgeon,
Joe Ranft, Chris Sanders, Domee Shi, and Nate Stanton
Back cover, clockwise from top left: Domee Shi, pen; Matthew
Luhn, digital; Joe Ranft, marker
Front flap: Jeff Pidgeon, marker
Back flap: Teddy Newton, marker
Title page: Matthew Luhn, digital

Manufactured in China

Jacket design by Liam Flanagan
Book design by Liam Flanagan and Neil Egan
Cover photograph by Deborah Coleman, Liam Flanagan, and
Neil Egan

10 9 8 7 6 5 4 3 2 1

Chronicle Books LLC
680 Second Street
San Francisco, California 94107
www.chroniclebooks.com

Contents

Foreword

At Pixar, every film we make is guided by the story's heart, by its core emotion. But as we work out a story, discovering its character development and the twists and turns of its plot, we also always keep an eye out for where the humor will be.

Humor is not just a funny line of dialogue that can be said by any character. True humor comes from character, from a character's unique personality and the character's reaction to a particular set of circumstances. It's no surprise, then, that story artists, with their incredible ability to bring characters and moments to vivid life, are often some of the funniest people you'll ever meet.

When you bring a group of story artists together into a single room, the result is magical. Whether they're meeting to discuss a scene in the movie, or just goofing around, raucous laughter echoes from the story room every day. I've always firmly believed that if you're having fun working on a film, that fun will come through on screen. And as you'll see in these pages . . . there's not a group at the studio that has more fun than the story department.

John Lasseter

Joe Ranft, marker,
pen, and pencil

Introduction

This book is filled with images you were never supposed to see. It's a chance to peek behind the curtain at the wonderful, sometimes weird process of creation at Pixar. The following pages showcase sketches, doodles, half-thoughts, crude one-liners, complete non sequiturs, and a handful of brilliant ideas that were not intended to be shared with anyone outside of the story room in which they were created. They were drawn to inspire—simple gags created to make the filmmakers, and ultimately the audience, laugh. This book celebrates the moment when a spark of an idea can take shape and grow into something the world can enjoy.

Every idea starts somewhere—Buzz and the gang crossing a busy road under orange traffic cones; Mrs. Incredible sailing her children to Nomanisan Island, her body stretched into the shape of a boat while her son's feet churn the open ocean like a propeller; or a monster emptying a full trash can onto a plate, turning the refuse into a gourmet lunch. Before these iconic moments made it to the screen, they existed as sketches, simple drawings created by skilled artists in the attempt to sell an idea. Often, in the development of our movies, the filmmakers will have a problem to solve or a moment in the movie that needs more entertainment. To remedy this issue, a team of artists (sometimes from across different departments throughout the company) will be assembled in the story room for what we affectionately call a "gag session." The goal of this meeting could be

quite broad—perhaps the director feels the second act needs more humor. Or it could be targeted—maybe trying to come up with fifty ways a room full of preschool toddlers could turn a toy's life into a living hell. Ideas fly fast and furious and if the room is successful, the director will walk away with something that is sure to make the movie stronger.

The term "gag session" is nothing new to animation. Filmmakers have been tasking groups of artists to come up with humorous ideas for cartoons since long before the first animated feature was created. Early animated shorts were merely a handful of gags strung together to form a loose storyline. Walt Disney was notorious for paying cash on the spot to the person with a session's best joke. Warner Bros' animation would host "No No Sessions," meetings in which people in the room were forbidden from saying "no" to any ideas (a tenet mirroring the "Yes, and" rule of acceptance in modern improv). At Pixar, the "gag session" follows our predecessors' examples. The funniest people in the company work together to solve a problem, committed to the belief that there are no bad ideas. The only rule is to try to make the person next to you laugh. Anything goes, and many times gags that we deemed too "out there" when pitched made it into the final film with great success (Buzz Lightyear switching to "Spanish mode" comes to mind). It's a shotgun approach to problem solving and a wonderfully spontaneous brain dump of creation. Having been lucky enough to be in the room for many sessions myself, I can tell you they are one of my favorite parts of the story process. I love the energy of a group of artists building off each other's ideas with a hive mind level of efficiency. Egos are checked at the door and most of the time no one can recall the origin of a gag. I might get a laugh for a drawing that was inspired by something another artist said in reaction to a third artist's doodle. A "gag session" is a true team effort and a heck of a lot of fun.

In your hands you hold a snapshot of the Pixar story process in its purest form, revealing the sometimes crude, but often hilarious path to creating our films. It's an opportunity to recognize the artists, many unseen, who lay the foundation of the studios' sense of humor. It's a chance to see a handful of gags, most of which were destined for the trash, but gave life to some of our proudest moments.

Welcome to the Pixar story room.
Jason Katz

Jason Katz, pencil

Joe Ranft, marker

THIS PAGE
Jason Katz and Robert Lence,
marker and pencil

TOY STORY

**Chris Sanders,
china marker**

A gag session isn't the sort of thing I'd volunteer for, as I don't see myself as a particularly funny person in a room. I'm the guy that thinks of something funny to say about three hours after a party has ended. But this particular situation in *Toy Story* was different—I lit up when I saw it. Claw games fascinate me: so many little happy, fuzzy, colorful things trapped inside a brightly lit prison, waiting for a notoriously unreliable claw to pluck them from the mob. How lucky the chosen one must feel. And how melancholy the ones left behind must be. To be dropped into that place like Buzz was, would be like landing in a little tub of madness.
—Chris Sanders

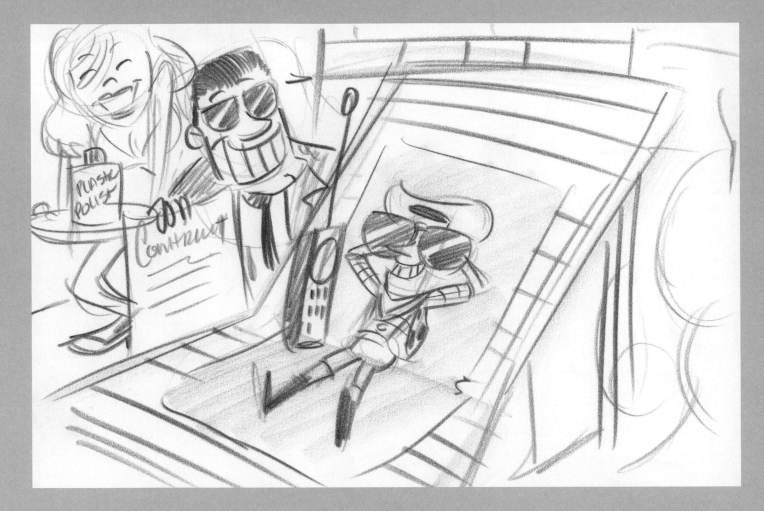

Ken Mitchroney, pencil

Jeff Pidgeon, marker

GUMBALL MACHINES

POP!

CRANK

(A)

(B)

BOING!

WOODY
JACK IN THE BOX
IN CACTUS

THIS SPREAD
Matthew Luhn, marker and pencil

Matthew Luhn, pen and pencil

Matthew Luhn, pen

LEFT
Matthew Luhn,
pen and colored pencil

OPPOSITE
Jason Katz,
marker and colored pencil

Bobby Podesta, pencil and marker

I just become lifeless everytime
my "kid" enters the room.

Teddy Newton, pencil

"the box"   lunchbox in the hot sun

Jeff Pidgeon, marker

Teddy Newton, pencil

Jeff Pidgeon, marker

Jeff Pidgeon, marker

Matthew Luhn, marker
and colored pencil

ABOVE
Jeff Pidgeon, china marker

RIGHT
Jeff Pidgeon, marker

DIALOGUE: GAMEBOY: ♪♪ A TEAM OF FORTY JAPANESE COMPUTER SCIENTISTS DIDN'T ENGINEER ME TO BECOME A CHEW TOY!!! ♪♪

Adrian Molina, pencil

Matthew Luhn, digital

Alien 'convicts'

Sippy cup
rattling
itself
against bars

THIS PAGE
Jeff Pidgeon, digital

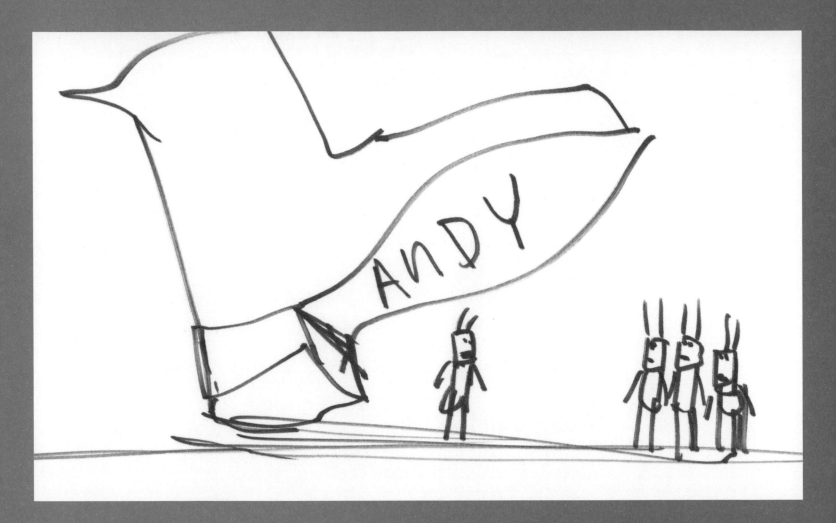

Joe Ranft, marker

Joe Ranft, pen and colored pencil

Joe Ranft always had a wonderfully macabre sense of humor and his drawing of Heimlich being sliced and diced by the Blueberries highlights this. The drawing ultimately inspired Joe's storyboards for the scene in which the ants welcomed the "warrior bugs" with a mural depicting the upcoming battle with the grasshoppers. Heimlich's death served a dramatic highlight. Contrasting the honest reality of life in the insect kingdom with the more lighthearted, family-friendly world of *A Bug's Life* never failed to make us laugh. The story room was often littered with drawings of one character gruesomely eating another. —Jason Katz

Bob Peterson, pen and colored pencil

THIS PAGE
Joe Ranft, pen and
colored pencil

Jason Katz, pen and colored pencil

Bob Peterson, pen and colored pencil

This drawing of Flik as adventurer was not a design assignment for me. Instead, I needed to create his gear as part of a sequence I was storyboarding where Flik leaves the colony. I tried to find a balance between cool and dorky. His garb, gathered from nature, covered the bases of food, shade, and defense. I really like the hat I created for him which was a bit conquistador, but also had a mad Napoleon shape to it. —Bob Peterson

aphids

cool
squeese
machine →

↓ juice

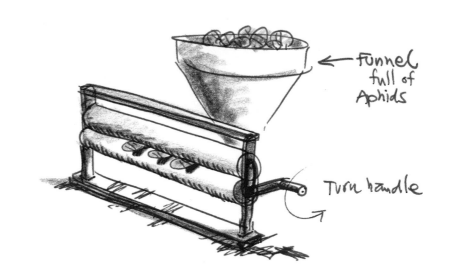

← funnel
full of
Aphids

Turn handle

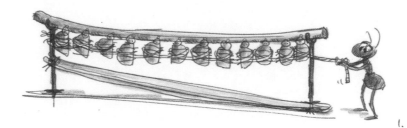

1.

2.

THIS PAGE
Jorgen Klubien, pen
and colored pencil

– could be connected to Bill Cone's wind mill

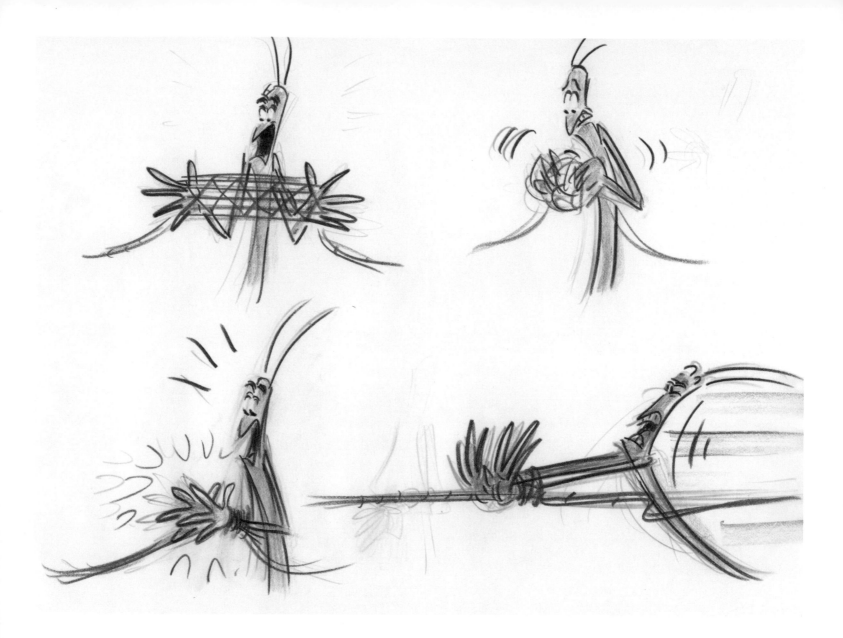

Jason Katz, colored pencil

THIS SPREAD
Robert Lence, watercolor, pencil, and marker

Jason Katz, pen and colored pencil

Jason Katz, pen and colored pencil

Jeff Pidgeon, pen and pencil

Nate Stanton, pen and colored pencil

Jason Katz, pen and pencil

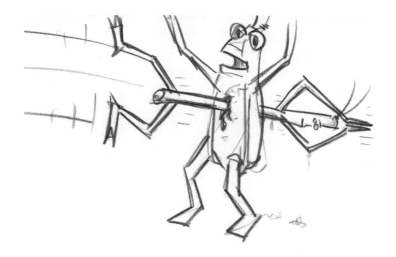

Dave Feiten, colored pencil

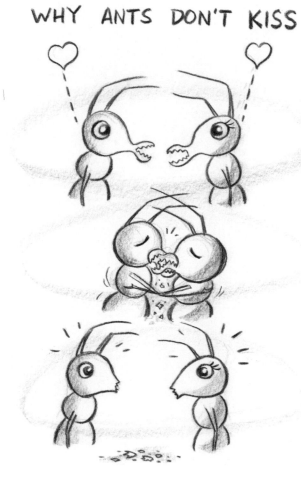

WHY ANTS DON'T KISS

Rob Gibbs, pencil

Jason Katz, pen and pencil

Jason Katz, pen, marker, and colored pencil

Bob Peterson, pen and pencil

Bob Pauley, pencil

STREET MUSICIAN

Bob Pauley, pen

Matthew Luhn and Max Brace, pen and pencil

Rob Gibbs, pencil

OPPOSITE, CLOCKWISE
FROM TOP LEFT
Bob Peterson, pen and pencil
Rob Gibbs, marker
Rob Gibbs, pencil
Bob Peterson, pen and pencil

Monsters, Inc. was a fun assignment because it juxtaposed the most mundane things in our human world with an exotic, yet goofy monster twist. Although, the newspaper tabloids were an interesting challenge because they were already filled with things that rival the craziness of the monster world! Just for the record, my mother in law is not a monster. And is not me. —Bob Peterson

CLOCKWISE FROM TOP LEFT
Bob Peterson, marker
Bob Peterson, marker and colored pencil
Rob Gibbs, china marker and colored pencil

Ted Mathot, marker and colored pencil

MONSTERS, INC.

The ultimate result of the eye-gag escalation

MONSTERS

OPPOSITE
Jason Katz, pen, marker
and colored pencil

LEFT
Jeff Pidgeon, marker

Matthew Luhn, pen and colored pencil

Matthew Luhn, pen and colored pencil

We have a "pee" gag in almost all of our Pixar movies! Remember Pearl the octopus inking herself in *Finding Nemo*? Or the Yeti offering Mike and Sulley yellow snow cones in *Monsters, Inc.?* Or Mater saying "He did what in his cup?" when Lightning McQueen explains the Piston Cup in *Cars*? You know urine a great company when pee gags are still funny. —Matthew Luhn

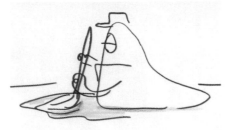

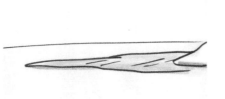

Matthew Luhn, pen and colored pencil

Monster BART train

Vampire taxi

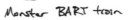

Jeff Pidgeon, pen

MONSTERS
UNIVERSITY

Mike
overdoes
the swag

Jeff Pidgeon, marker

Matthew Luhn, digital

THIS PAGE
Jeff Pidgeon, marker

Matthew Luhn, digital

M.U.
Glee
club

GO
TEAM
GO!

OPPOSITE, CLOCKWISE
FROM TOP LEFT
Jason Deamer, marker,
Jeff Pidgeon, marker

ABOVE
Jeff Pidgeon, marker

RIGHT
Matthew Luhn, digital

Matthew Luhn, digital

The salsa contact eye gag was an idea first pitched by Jason Katz on *Monsters, Inc.* The gag never made it into the film, but I thought it was hilarious, so I tried to pitch it again on *Monsters University.* It's common at Pixar for us to take unused gags from one film and insert them into another. Good ideas always seem to find a way of resurfacing. —Matthew Luhn

Monsters
University
traditions

Outside

Inside

SNAKE MONSTER SHEDS SKIN

...AND STREAKS!

ABOVE
Matthew Luhn, digital

LEFT
Kelsey Mann, digital

Panty raid

Creating a diversionary Prank

↑
Real prank

↑
diversion

ABOVE
Jeff Pidgeon, marker

TOP RIGHT
Adrian Molina, marker and pencil

RIGHT
Adrian Molina, pencil

Sully uses
Mike scare
cans to drink
ooze soda from

THIS PAGE
Matthew Luhn, digital

OPPOSITE
Jeff Pidgeon, marker and
colored pencil

Cramming with multiple books

Jeff Pidgeon, marker

Jeff Pidgeon, marker

Adrian Molina, marker

Sometimes you just have to give your brain the problem and get out of the way. Crabacus is the direct result of zero editing and zero shame. You put your head down, draw the picture, and hope somebody laughs when you reveal it. —Adrian Molina

"CHICKENFISH"

OPPOSITE
Dan Jeup, pencil and marker

The Tank Gang were grown in fish tanks to sell along with aquariums. They knew more about people than about being ocean fish. Of course, they were limited to the dentist, his patients, and whatever was onscreen in the waiting room. We storyboarded whole sequences where the gang waited for their favorite soap opera to come on and it would be about any or all soap tropes. Easy now to imagine why the members of The Tank Gang are rather melodramatic and hammy. —Ronnie del Carmen

LEFT
Ricky Nierva,
colored pencil

Ralph Eggleston, marker

CLOCKWISE FROM TOP LEFT
Jason Katz, marker ,
Jason Katz, china marker and colored pencil,
Jason Katz, marker
Ricky Nierva, marker,

Unknown artist, pen

Joseph "Rocket" Ekers, pen and colored pencil

Jeff Pidgeon, marker

THIS PAGE
Bruce Morris, pen and pencil

RIGHT
Bruce Morris, pen and pencil

BOTTOM LEFT
Jason Katz, marker

BOTTOM RIGHT
Matthew Luhn, marker

MERRY GO ROUND

WHEEEE!!

WHEEE!! WHEEE!!

FAMILY OF STARFISH GOING TO SCHOOL.

Jason Katz, china marker and colored pencil

CLOCKWISE FROM TOP LEFT
Matthew Luhn, marker; Jeff Pidgeon, marker; Matthew Luhn, pen;
Jason Katz, china marker and colored pencil.

THIS SPREAD
Teddy Newton, marker

THIS SPREAD
Teddy Newton, marker

FROZONE
COOLS
THE
BEERS.

Teddy Newton, marker

Geefwee Boedoe, marker

THIS PAGE
Teddy Newton,
marker

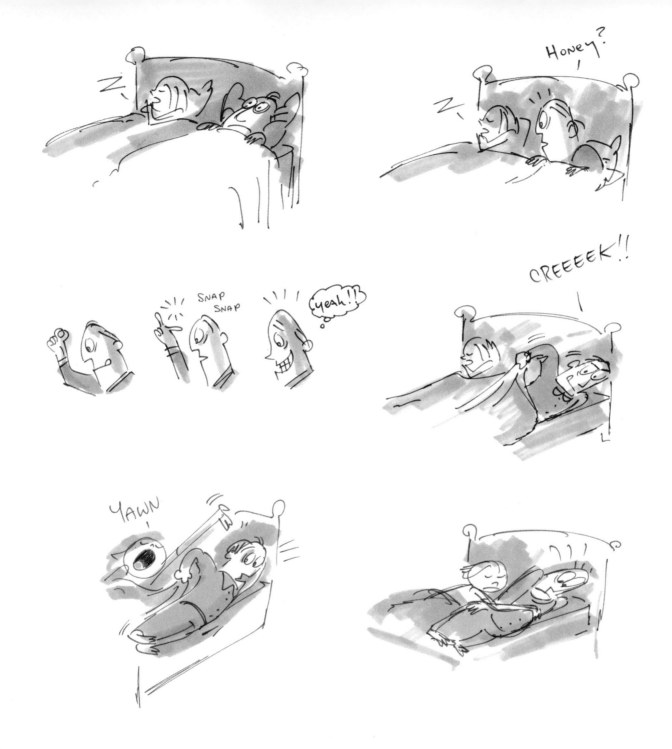

THE INCREDIBLES

ZIP!!

SMACK!!

Teddy Newton, pen and marker

THE INCREDIBLES

THE INCREDIBLES

IT'S A
SUCCESS!!

THIS SPREAD
Teddy Newton, marker

The secret to a great story gag has less to do with its novelty and more to do with the truth it possesses. To me, the funniest moments in *The Incredibles* are not the outrageous bits of spectacle, but the banal moments we recognize from our own lives. —Teddy Newton

Teddy Newton, marker

Max Brace, marker

Teddy Newton, marker

Matthew Luhn, marker and colored pencil

He must be on that new health kick!

CAR JUNK FOOD

Rusty Nut KABOB

Greesy Lug Nuts

Hot Sludge
(served in Funnle)

I'm So Embarrassed

ESPRESSO 10W40

CLOCKWISE FROM TOP LEFT
Teddy Newton, marker
Rob Gibbs, colored pencil
Matthew Luhn, colored pencil
Rob Gibbs, pencil

NUDE CAR BEACH

THIS PAGE
Teddy Newton, marker

Though a director must stay on point with their picture, a good gagman can generally inspire that director with an unexpected drawing. Sometimes an irreverent idea, which may never end up in the final film, has the ability to prompt that "eureka!" moment every creative person lives for. —Teddy Newton

Monster Truck

Teddy Newton, marker

"HAVE A MINT."

Teddy Newton, marker

Rob Gibbs, china marker

JACKELOPE
CROSSING

Bud Luckey, pencil

Brian Fee, pencil

Bobby Podesta,
marker

Erik Benson, marker

Jeff Pidgeon, marker

Say Ahh!

Teddy Newton, marker

Mother of All CARS

Teddy Newton, marker

Teddy Newton, marker

Rob Gibbs, marker

Unknown artist, marker

Rob Gibbs, pencil

Teddy Newton, marker

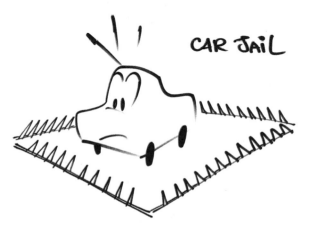

Josh Cooley, marker and pencil

wind Power

MOUTH MISSILE

DRIVE BY MOONING

AXLEROD CHRISTENS A SHIP.

CLOCKWISE FROM TOP LEFT
Rob Gibbs, pencil
Josh Cooley, pencil
Josh Cooley, pencil
Josh Cooley, marker

THIS PAGE
Erik Benson, pen

These handcrafted drawings were made with thousands of hours of meticulous focus and dedication. I think the beauty speaks for itself. —Erik Benson

Hipster Mater

Filmore Mater

Time machine Mater

That chair Mater

The table over there Mater

Invisible Mater

Derek Thompson, pen and pencil

Scott Morse, pen

Kevin O'Brien, marker and colored pencil

OPPOSITE
Matthew Luhn, digital

THIS PAGE
Matthew Luhn, pen and
colored pencil

SCARING
TOURISTS AT THE CATACOMBS

Jim Capobianco, pen and pencil

Jeff Pidgeon, marker

RIGHT
Harley Jessup,
pen, marker, and
colored pencil

CHAIR IDEAS

HIGHTOP SNEAKER

CHAMPAGNE CORK

FERRY

COUNTER-WEIGHTED ELEVATOR

Matthew Luhn, digital

teeter
totter
chopping

Matthew Luhn, digital

Matthew Luhn, pen, marker, and pencil

Matthew Luhn, pen, marker, and pencil

CAN'T STAND SEWER SMELL

THIS PAGE
Matthew Luhn, digital

ABOVE
Jason Deamer, marker

TOP RIGHT AND RIGHT
Matthew Luhn, digital

"DEVELOPMENT"

SCENE #   DATE   ARTIST   PANEL #

DIALOGUE:

OPPOSITE AND ABOVE
Jeff Pidgeon, marker

"Day at Work"

Max Brace, pen and marker

Jeff Pidgeon, marker

"DEVELOPMENT"

DIALOGUE:

Jim Reardon, marker

tap tap

THIS SPREAD
Jeff Pidgeon, marker

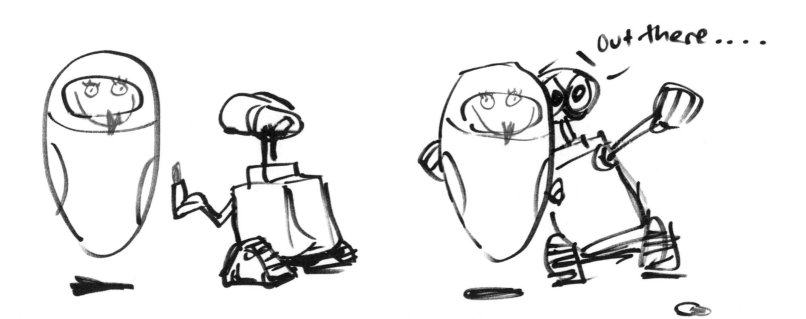

1

2

3

4

THIS SPREAD
Jeff Pidgeon, marker

This series of gags comes from a classic short film structure called "Try and Fail." Sometimes the main character comes up with a series of ideas to achieve his/her goal, and sometimes an instruction book is used to set up each "Try." When EVE goes into shutdown mode, I thought WALL·E could dig up an old "How to Be Romantic" book and try to coax her out. My thought was that some of the humor and charm would come from the fact that WALL·E would only have trash items at his disposal! —Jeff Pidgeon

oversized
collar

Wally
pokes at captain's
fat

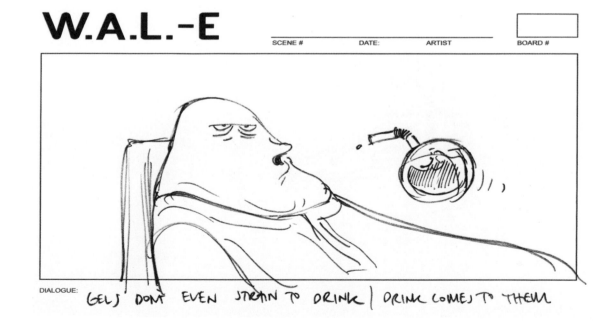

W.A.L.-E

SCENE #   DATE: ARTIST   BOARD #

DIALOGUE: GELS DONT EVEN STRAIN TO DRINK | DRINK COMES TO THEM

ABOVE
Jeff Pidgeon, pen

RIGHT
Nate Stanton, pen

Toilet Bot

stylist bot

TOP LEFT
Jim Reardon, pen

ABOVE
Jeff Pidgeon, china marker

LEFT
Jim Reardon, marker

W.A.L.-E

SCENE #   DATE: ARTIST   BOARD #

DIALOGUE:

THIS PAGE
Jeff Pidgeon, pen

his wife dies

Teddy Newton, marker

Patrick McDonnell, pen and watercolor

Pete Docter, marker and colored pencil

This was the first drawing I did after Bob Peterson and I talked of doing a film about a grouchy old man. The fact that he sold happy, fun, colorful balloons seemed like a funny contrast to his demeanor—and also helped explain where he gets the goods to float his house. —Pete Docter

Pete Docter, marker

I did a whole series of scribbles like these, exploring Carl's habits and mannerisms, trying to get a handle on who he was before we wrote the script.
—Pete Docter

THIS PAGE
Teddy Newton, pen

Teddy Newton, marker

Teddy Newton, pen and marker

Teddy Newton, pen

Teddy Newton, pen and marker

Matthew Luhn, pen and pencil

Teddy Newton, pen

Ken Bruce, pen and pencil

THIS PAGE
Jeff Pidgeon, marker

THIS PAGE
Jeff Pidgeon, marker

OPPOSITE
Peter Sohn, pen

ABOVE
Teddy Newton, marker

RIGHT
Jeff Pidgeon, marker

OPPOSITE
Jeff Pidgeon, china marker

TOP LEFT AND LEFT
Jeff Pidgeon, marker

TOP RIGHT
Jeff Pidgeon, pencil

ABOVE
Erik Benson, pencil

Healing Bear crystals

Bear home security system

Bear pipes

Bear stress ball

Bear catcher

Bear 8 Ball

not likely

Bear muffs

Bear stein

Bear attack mobile (head goes up + down!)

THIS PAGE
Erik Benson, pencil

These are souvenirs for the old witch's hut in *Brave*. Inspired by the many quality items I have purchased at old witch's huts inside airports. —Erik Benson

How would Merida's brothers scare or distract the guards in order for Merida and her mother to escape? That was the challenge for these gags, with the limitation of what would be available as props and settings in a medieval-like castle. —Valerie LaPointe

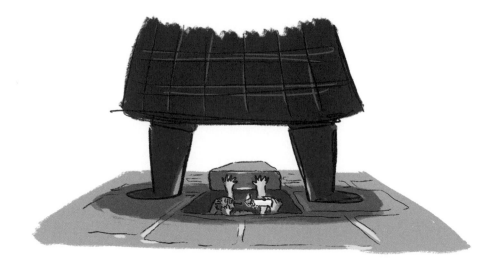

THIS PAGE
Jeff Pidgeon, china
marker and marker

Jeff Pidgeon, china marker

SADNESS WEARS MOM JEANS.

Josh Cooley, marker and pencil

THIS PAGE
Daniel Chong, marker

Sadness wears
hazmat
suit
so she can
hold memories

Daniel Chong, pen

Unknown artist, pencil

THIS PAGE
Tony Fucile, pencil

Domee Shi, pen

You never see it onscreen, but most of the
imaginary boyfriends Joy created to get
back to Headquarters must have ended up in
the Memory Dump. In the story room, we felt
bad about that until we remembered . . . they
would die for Riley. And they're imaginary.
—Josh Cooley

Tony Fucile, pencil

Angor sometimes rips off his shirt

Daniel Chong, marker

Yung-Han Chang, marker

RIGHT
Domee Shi, marker

BELOW
Tony Rosenast, pen

FEAR gets into recall unit his butt gets projected on the screen

CUT to Riley singing "Butt" song

♫ Butt, ♪ Butt, ♫ Butt

MO-CAP DREAMS

Valerie LaPointe, pen and watercolor

Riley's story shifted a lot in the early stages of developing *Inside Out*. One of my particular favorites was when it was about Riley's relationship with her long-time best friend. I drew ideas directly from my own memories of playing with my close friends and cousins when I was young. Small, humorous moments are often the best way to make a character specific and original. —Valerie LaPointe

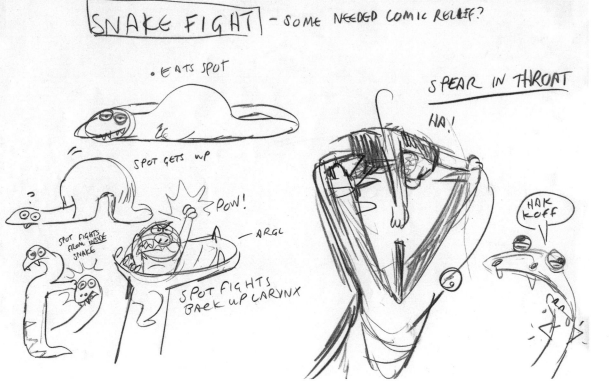

SNAKE FIGHT — SOME NEEDED COMIC RELIEF?

• EATS SPOT

SPOT GETS UP

SPOT FIGHTS FROM INSIDE SNAKE

POW!

— ARGL

SPOT FIGHTS BACK UP LARYNX

SPEAR IN THROAT

HA!

HAK KOFF

LEFT
J.P. Vine, pencil

BELOW
Louise Smythe,
digital

OPPOSITE
Kelsey Mann, marker

This is the first gag drawing I ever did on the show. I was searching for entertaining ways to see Arlo helping out on the farm. I have no idea why I thought he would have hands with fingers. With gag drawings, it's more about the idea and the joke. At least that's what I keep telling people to avoid them realizing that I'm just plain lazy. —Kelsey Mann

Scared of Dino Chickens

Erik Benson, digital

Erik Benson, digital

Erik Benson, digital

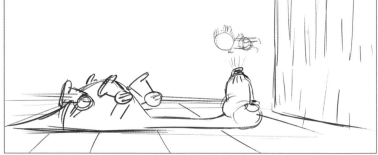

Edgar Karapetyan, digital

Push trees over
like lumberjacks

ABOVE
Louise Smythe, digital

RIGHT
Erik Benson, pencil

Austin Madison, digital

"THAT CAME OUT OF *WHERE?*"

LEFT
Mark Walsh, marker and pencil

We struggled with the humans for a long time. As you do in story, you explore all avenues. Like the one where dinosaurs keep humans locked up in cages and poke at them with spears in a rhythmic pattern to make their screams produce music. Come to think of it, I'm not sure why we didn't go this route. Kids love human torture. —Kelsey Mann

SPOT POST
RUSTLER
FIGHT

Kelsey Mann, marker

Mark Walsh, marker

Ting!

Valerie LaPointe, digital

HIDE + GO SEEK

Rosana Sullivan, digital

Gleb Sanchez-Lobashov, digital

THIS PAGE
Gleb Sanchez-Lobashov, digital

SPOT EATS
THE TICKS

ARLO TRIES TO
FIND TICKS IN SPOT

Acknowledgments

Thanks to all of the filmmakers who ever did battle behind the Pixar story room doors:

Mark Andrews
Kelly Asbury
Robert Baird
James Baker
Erik Benson
Randy Berrett
Brad Bird
Geefwee Boedoe
Courtney Booker
Rejean Bourdages
Steve Boyett
Max Brace
Colin Brady
Ash Brannon
Ken Bruce
Mike Cachuela
Adam Campbell
Jim Capobianco
Doug Carney
Enrico Casarosa
Yung-Han Chang
Brenda Chapman
Daniel Chong
Emma Coats
Josh Cooley
Jill Culton
Ricardo Curtis
Elias Davis
Jason Deamer

Ronnie Del Carmen
Pete Docter
Don Dougherty
Everett Downing
Ralph Eggleston
Joseph "Rocket" Ekers
Perry Farinola
Brian Fee
Dave Feiten
Doug Frankel
Tony Fucile
David Fulp
Daniel Gerson
Rob Gibbs
Louis Gonzales
Dalton Grant
Craig Grasso
Stephen "Toaster" Gregory
Kirk Hanson
Tasha Harris
Jimmy Hayward
Manny Hernandez
John Hoffman
Mark Holmes
Sam Hood
Justin Hunt
Steven Hunter
Harley Jessup
Dan Jeup
Andrew Jimenez
Trevor Jimenez
Barry Johnson
Matt Jones

Edgar Karapetyan
Jason Katz
Charles Keagle
Dean Kelly
Jorgen Klubien
Vlad Kooperman
Valerie LaPointe
Brian Larsen
John Lasseter
Dan Lee
Robert Lence
Kristen Lester
Brad Lewis
Bud Luckey
Matthew Luhn
Jeffrey Lynch
Angus MacLane
Lauren MacMullan
Austin Madison
Tony Maki
Kelsey Mann
Max Martinez
Ted Mathot
Patrick McDonnell
Nathaniel McLaughlin
Jon Mead
Paul Mica
Ken Mitchroney
Adrian Molina
Stanley Moore
Bruce Morris
Scott Morse
Teddy Newton

Bosco Ng
Ricky Nierva
Floyd Norman
Kevin O'Brien
Brian O'Connell
Chris O'Dowd
Sanjay Patel
Bob Pauley
Bob Peterson
Laura Phillips
Jeff Pidgeon
Jan Pinkava
Bobby Podesta
David Pollock
Karen Prell
Bill Presing
Steve Purcell
John Ramirez
Joe Ranft
Jim Reardon
David Reynolds
James Robertson
Octavio Rodriguez
Christian Roman
Lou Romano
Tony Rosenast
Bobby Rubio
Gleb Sanchez-Lobashov
Chris Sanders
John Sanford
Jeff Sangalli
Dan Scanlon
Gary Schultz

Bob Scott
Garett Sheldrew
Domee Shi
Kyle Shockley
Patrick Siemer
David Silverman
David Skelly
Louise Smythe
Peter Sohn
Andrew Stanton
Nate Stanton
Rosana Sullivan
Nick Sung
Doug Sweetland
Shion Takeuchi
Derek Thompson
Bud Thon
Lee Unkrich
J.P. Vine
Mark Walsh
Tasha Wedeen
Glenn Williamson
Alex Woo
Justin Wright
Michael Yates

Thanks to all of the creatives at Pixar
and Chronicle who crafted this book:

Kelly Bonbright
Lia Brown
Deborah Cichocki
Michelle Clair
Deborah Coleman
Michael Del Rosario
Courtney Drew
Andy Dreyfus
Neil Egan
Heather Feng
Liam Flanagan
Christine Freeman
Emily Haynes
Molly Jones
Jason Katz
Shana Levin
Matthew Luhn
LeighAnna MacFadden
Jeanette Marker
Karen Paik
Bowbay Pellicano
Jeff Pidgeon
Juliet Roth
Shiho Tilley
Melissa Woods

–Jason Katz

Floyd Norman, marker

Most cartoonists are first and foremost observers. We simply watch what happens around us and put it down on paper. I've been practicing this animation tradition since the sixties at the Walt Disney Studios and continued it when I moved to Pixar in 1997. This gag is based on my animation colleagues and what usually happens after a picture wraps: we forget all the arguments and fights and suddenly we're best friends again. —Floyd Norman